Big Machines in the City

by Brienna Rossiter

FOCUS READERS®

SCOUT

www.focusreaders.com

Focus Readers is distributed by North Star Editions:
sales@northstareditions.com | 888-417-0195

Produced for Focus Readers by Red Line Editorial.

Photographs ©: Shutterstock Images, cover, 1, 4 (top), 4 (bottom), 7, 9 (top), 9 (bottom), 11 (top), 11 (bottom), 13, 15 (top), 15 (bottom), 16 (top left), 16 (top right), 16 (bottom left), 16 (bottom right)

Library of Congress Cataloging-in-Publication Data
Names: Rossiter, Brienna, author.
Title: Big machines in the city / by Brienna Rossiter.
Description: Lake Elmo, MN : Focus Readers, [2021] | Series: Big machines |
    Includes index. | Audience: Grades K-1.
Identifiers: LCCN 2020033636 (print) | LCCN 2020033637 (ebook) | ISBN
    9781644936726 (hardcover) | ISBN 9781644937082 (paperback) | ISBN
    9781644937808 (pdf) | ISBN 9781644937440 (ebook)
Subjects: LCSH: Motor vehicles--Juvenile literature. | Railroad
    trains--Juvenile literature.
Classification: LCC TL147 .R655 2021 (print) | LCC TL147 (ebook) | DDC
    629.2--dc23
LC record available at https://lccn.loc.gov/2020033636
LC ebook record available at https://lccn.loc.gov/2020033637

Printed in the United States of America
Mankato, MN
012021

About the Author

Brienna Rossiter is a writer and editor who lives in Minnesota. She loves being outside, especially near the water.

Table of Contents

Trucks

Many trucks drive in the city.

Some trucks carry **mail**.

Some trucks carry big **loads**.

Garbage trucks pick up trash.

The trash goes to a **dump**.

trash

Tow trucks move cars.

Some tow trucks pull cars.

They use hooks.

Some tow trucks carry cars.

Buses

Buses carry people.

People sit or stand inside.

They move around the city.

Trains

Trains carry people, too.

Trains go on tracks.

Some tracks are up high.

Some trains are subways.

They use **tunnels**.

They go underground.

subway

tunnel

Glossary

dump

mail

loads

tunnels

Index